GEM User Manual

by
Kripa Shankar Sharma

Kindle Edition

* * * * *

Published by Kripa Shankar Sharma at Kindle

My Book
Copyright 2010 by Kripa Shankar Sharma

GEM User Manual

1) Login to GEM 3.0/2.0
2) We begin with GEM 3.0 as this one is currently in use and is more important to know and 2.0 is almost closed down.

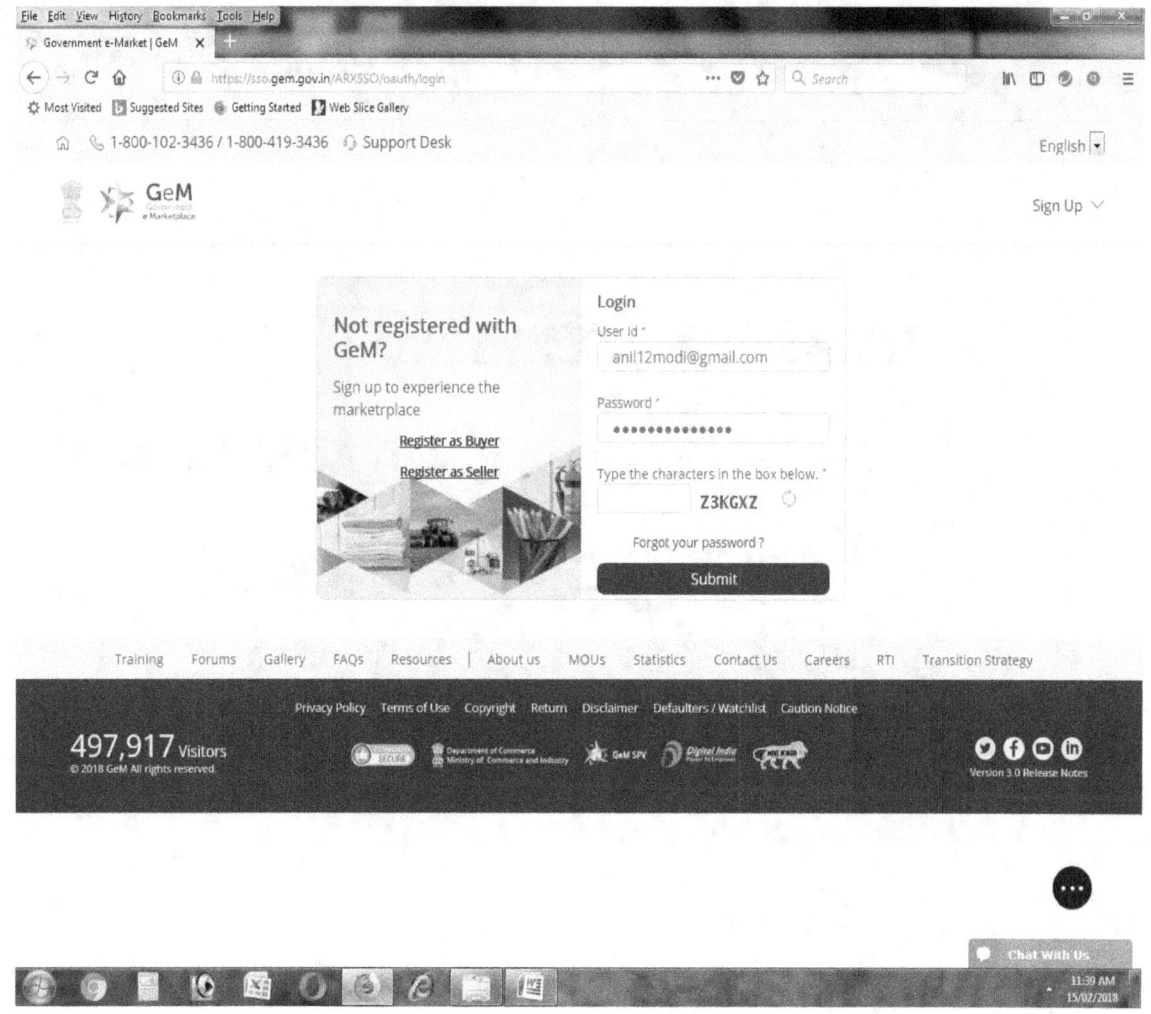

Enter the username, Password & the captcha correctly. Press enter or click on submit.

After logging in you get this screen

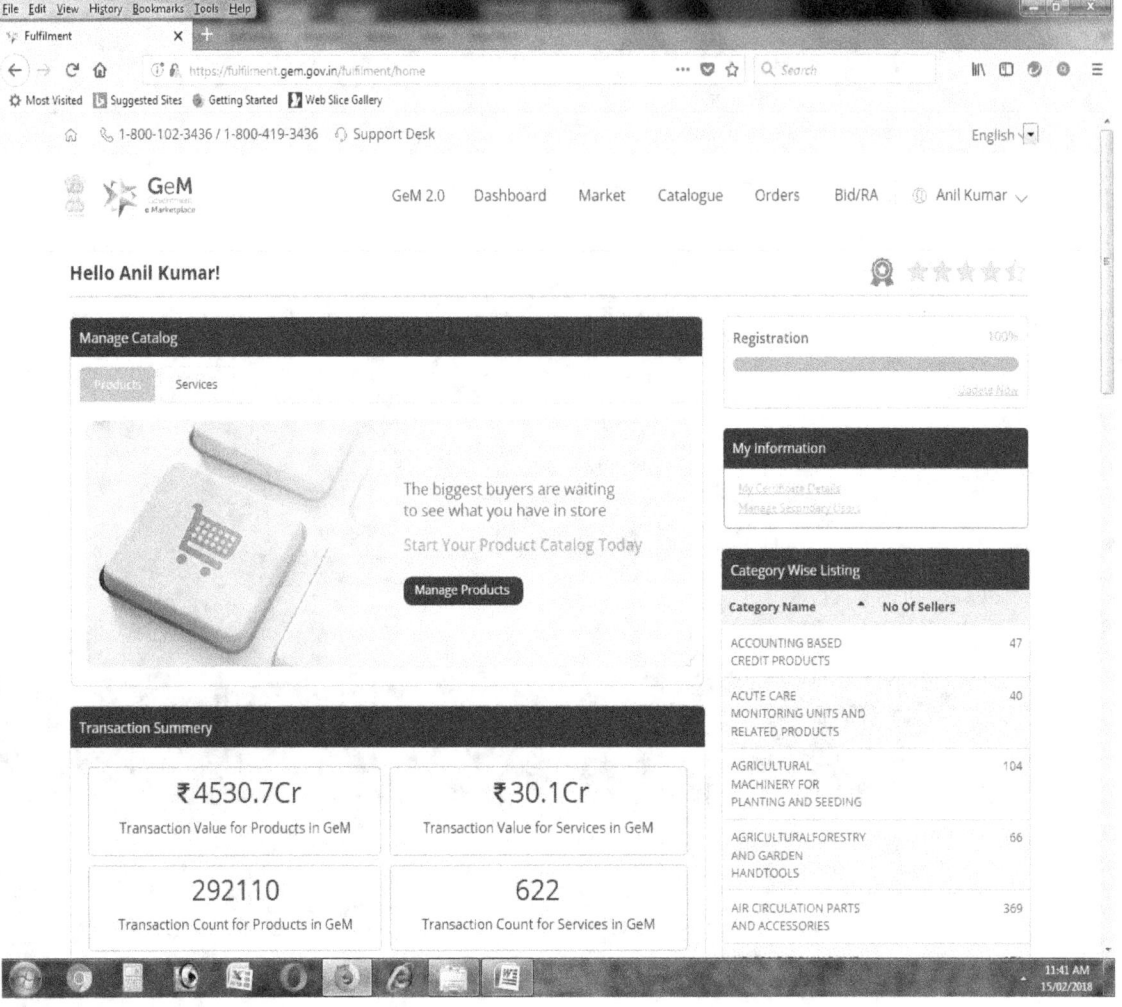

The above screen is called the dashboard

3) Market – In order to search for products you need to go to market link at the top of the page

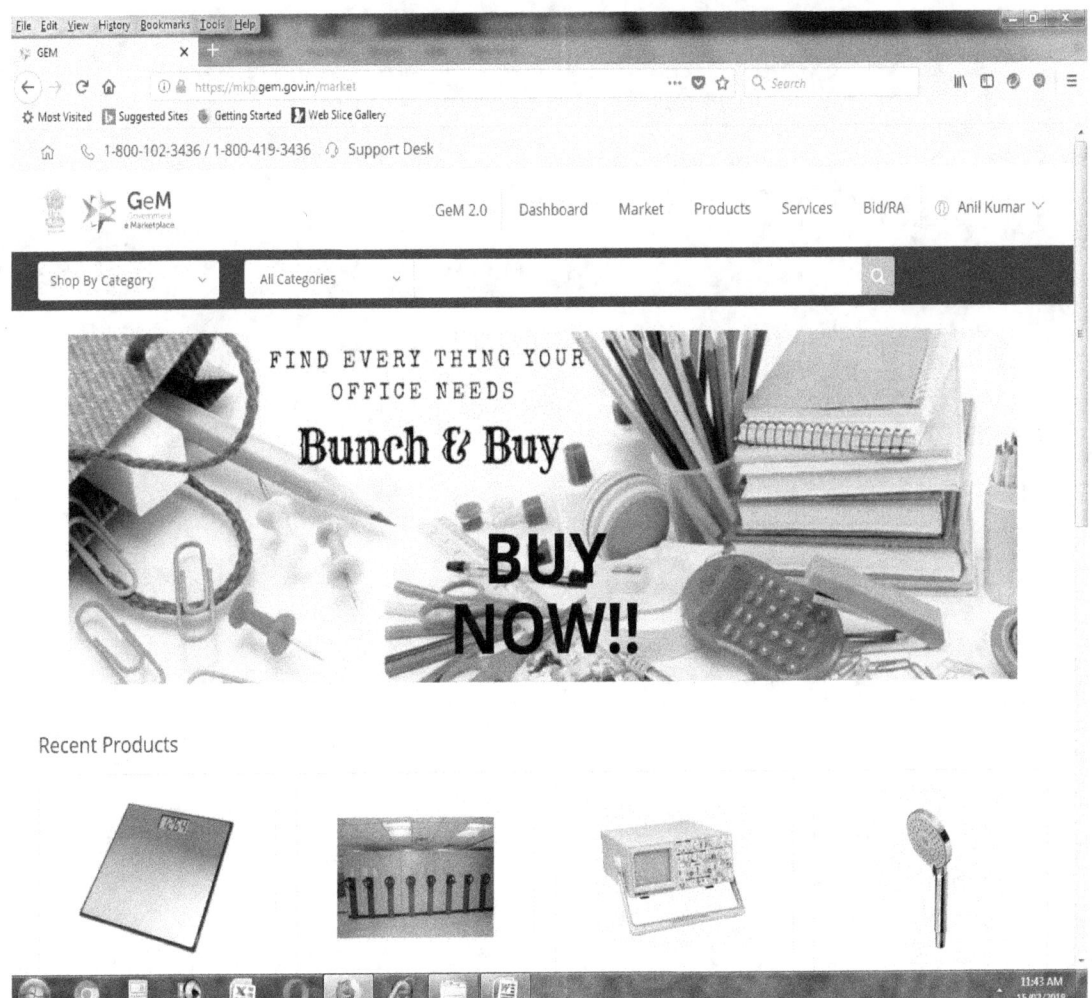

Type in the product you need to search I tried brother 2321d printer n got this:-

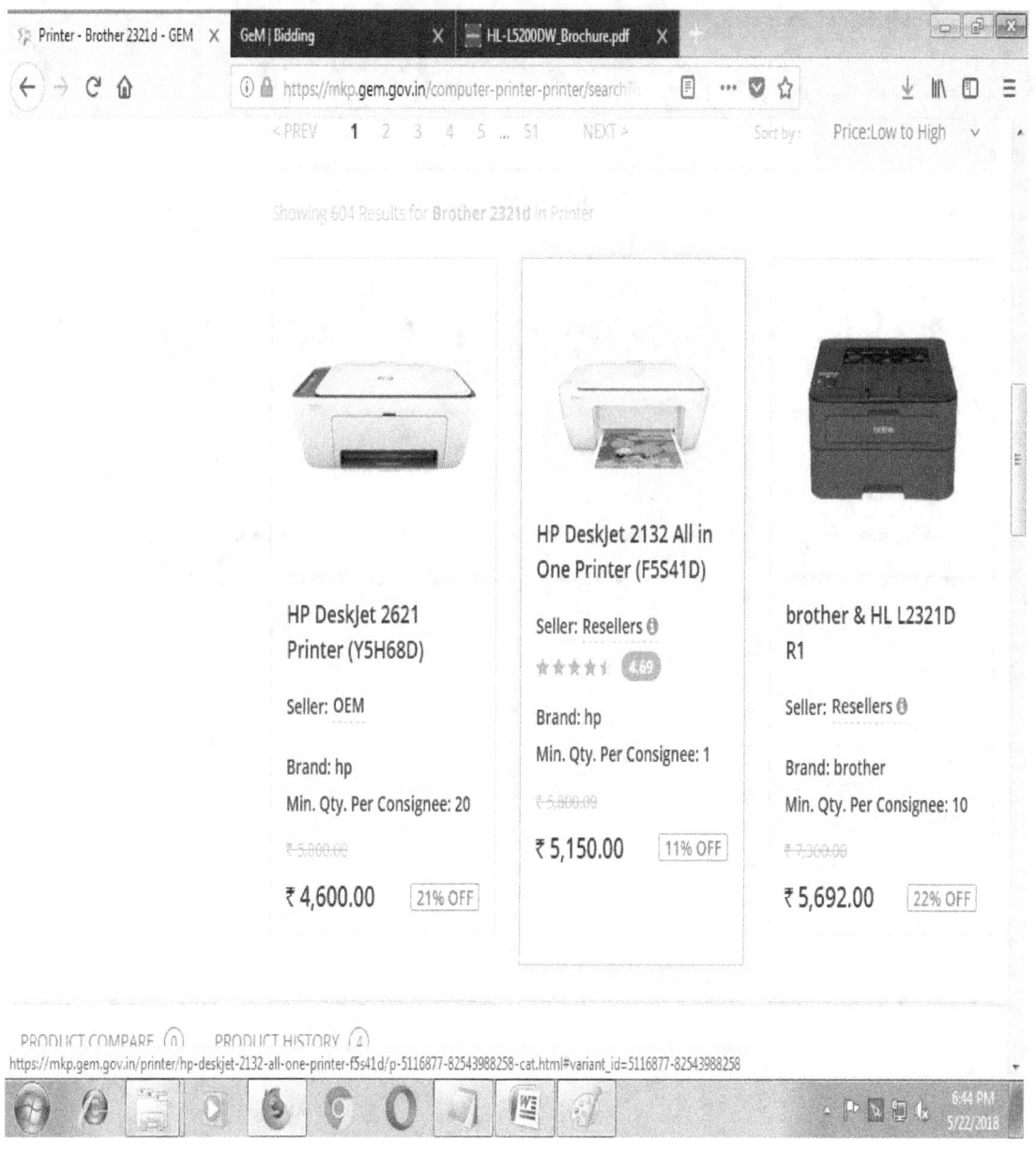

Now I can find multiple same products while searching in the market also check their specs and who is selling those products as well.

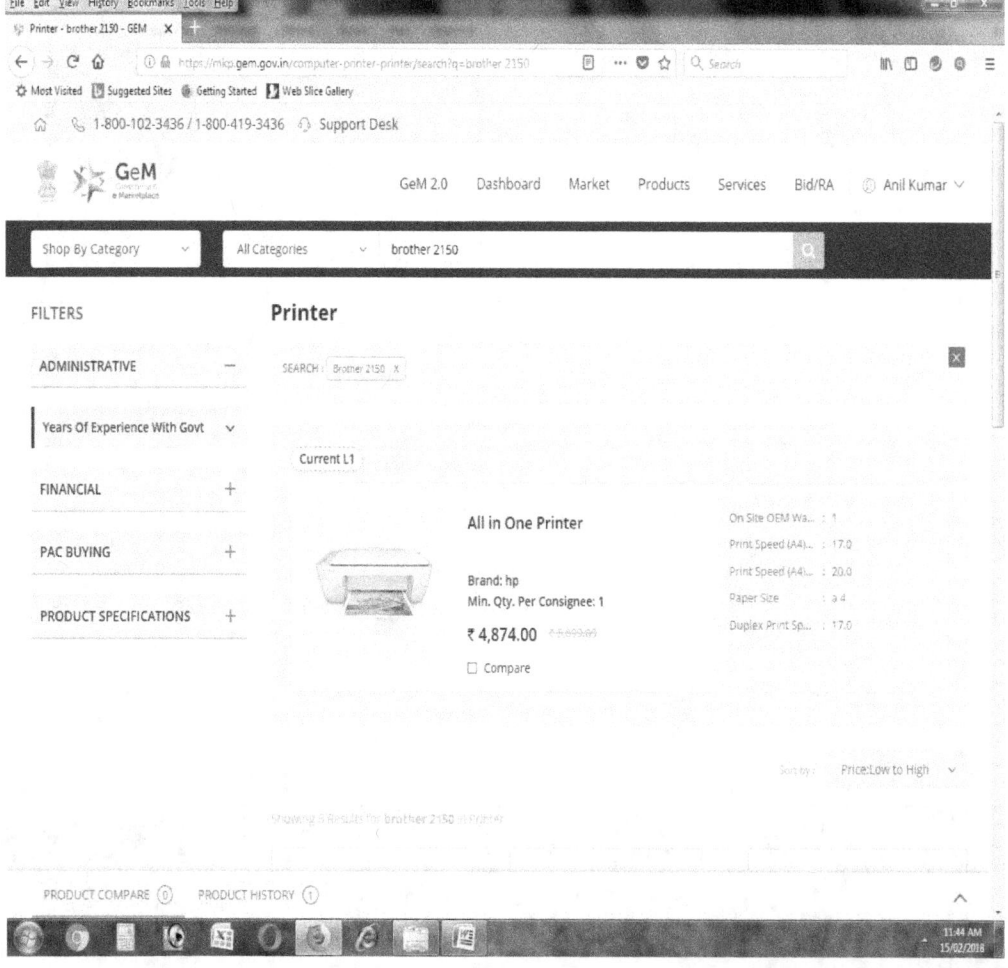

Here is the rest of it, you can also search by the specs of the product or by make and model where make is the brand of the product and model is like 2321d and ex for make Brother, HP, Lenovo etc.

BROTHER

Monochrome Laser Multi function Centres

Monochrome Laser Multi function Centres

Brand: brother
Min. Qty. Per Consignee: 2

Brand: brother
Min. Qty. Per Consignee: 2

Brand: brother
Min. Qty. Per Consignee: 1

₹ 6,350.00 28% OFF

₹ 11,408.00 24% OFF

₹ 14,255.01 11% OFF

☐ Compare

☐ Compare

☐ Compare

Monochrome Laser Multi function Centres

Brother FAX 2840

Monochrome Laser Multi function Centres

Brand: brother
Min. Qty. Per Consignee: 1

Brand: brother
Min. Qty. Per Consignee: 1

Brand: brother
Min. Qty. Per Consignee: 10

4) Catalog- It's the place to upload all your products
    a) These days in most of product cat. Only option to upload is to pair your product with someone else's upload and a new method of validating authorization has come into play which is called reseller panel procedure on next page

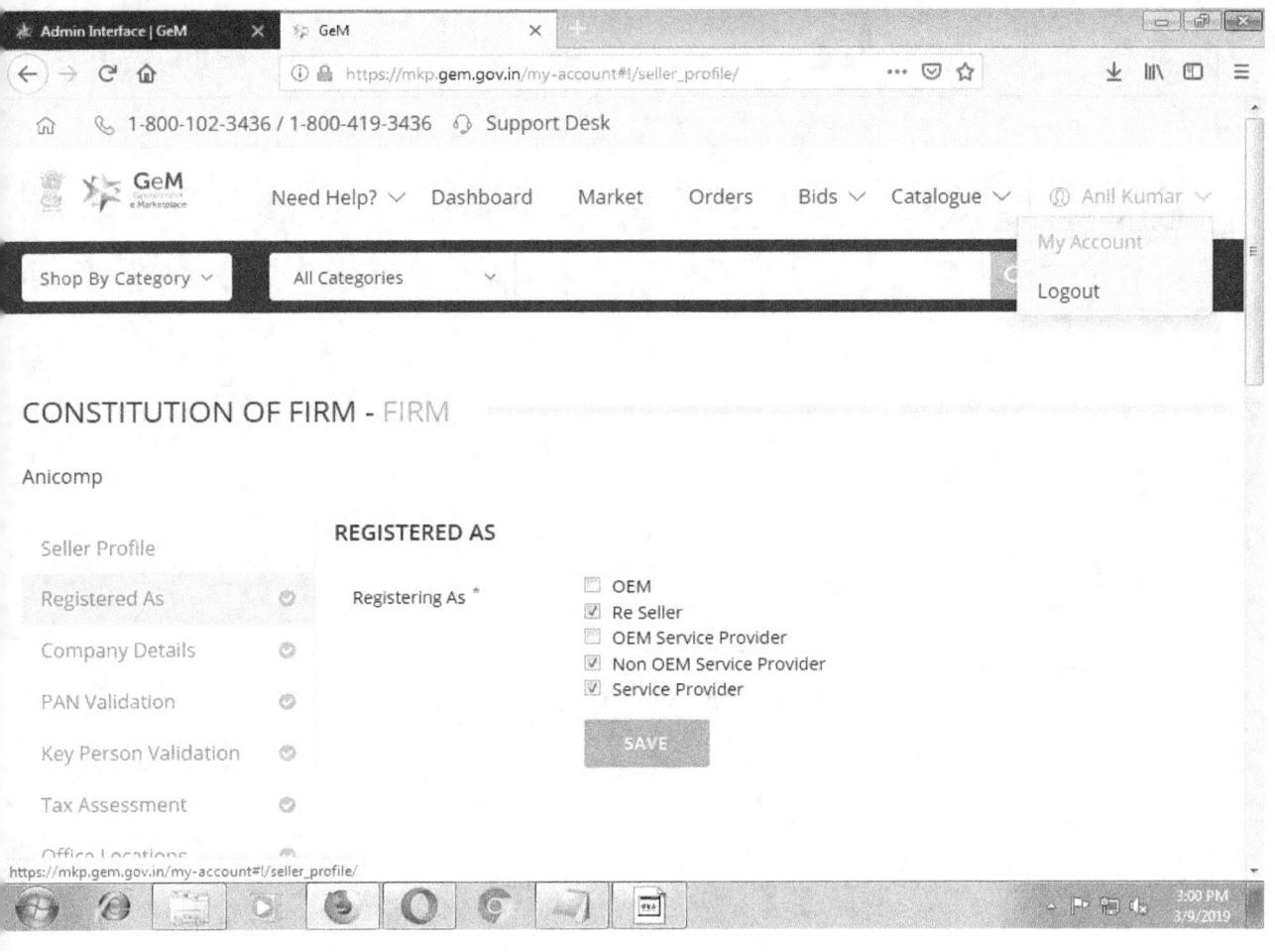

Click on your account name which in this case is Anil Kumar n then click **my account** now scroll down and click **Reseller Panel** which will look like this (next screen shot)

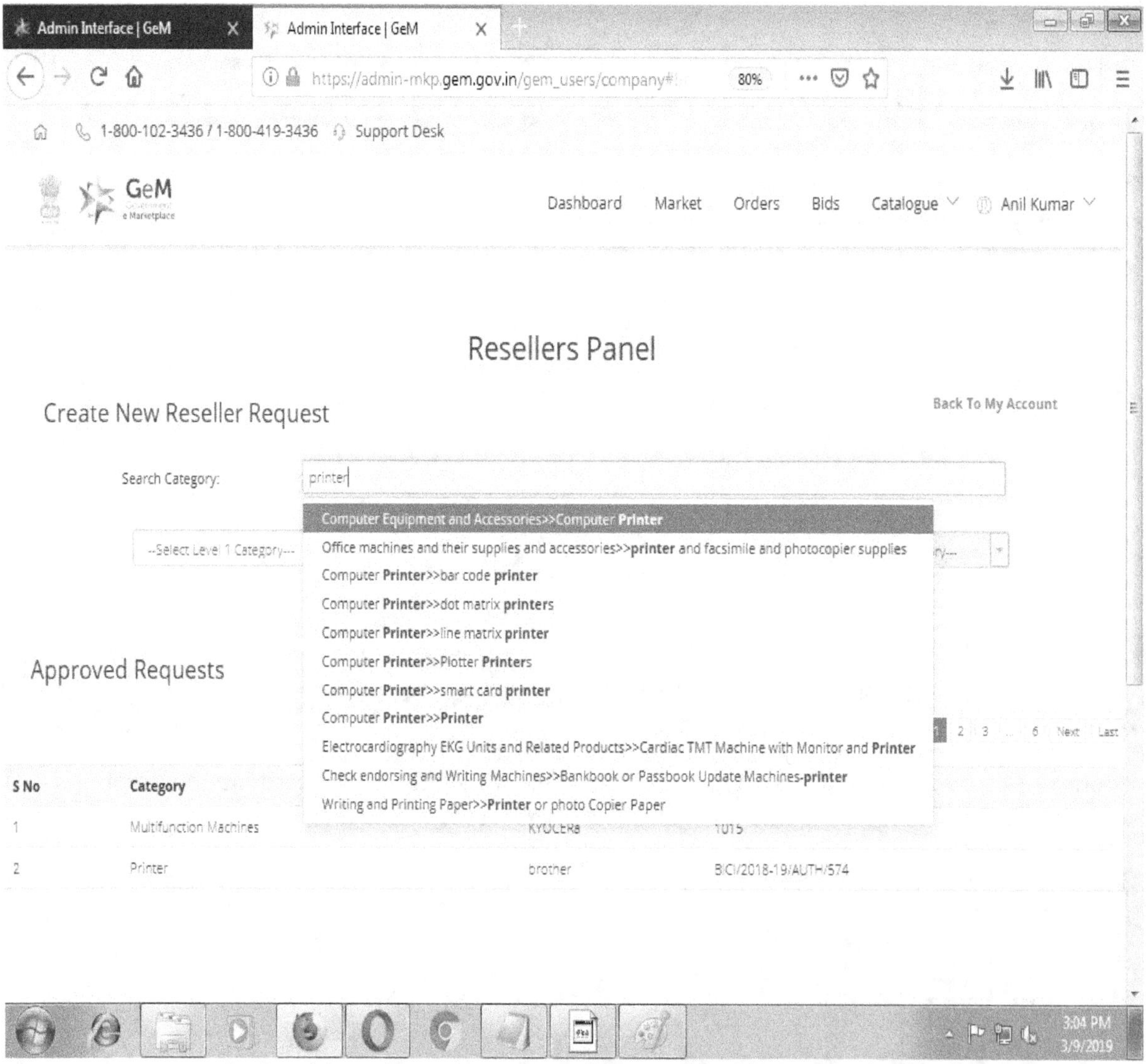

In the above picture I am at reseller panel and have searched for printer in reseller panel just like we do while uploading products then we choose the suitable product category and you will need the authorization letter from the OEM handy for doing this.

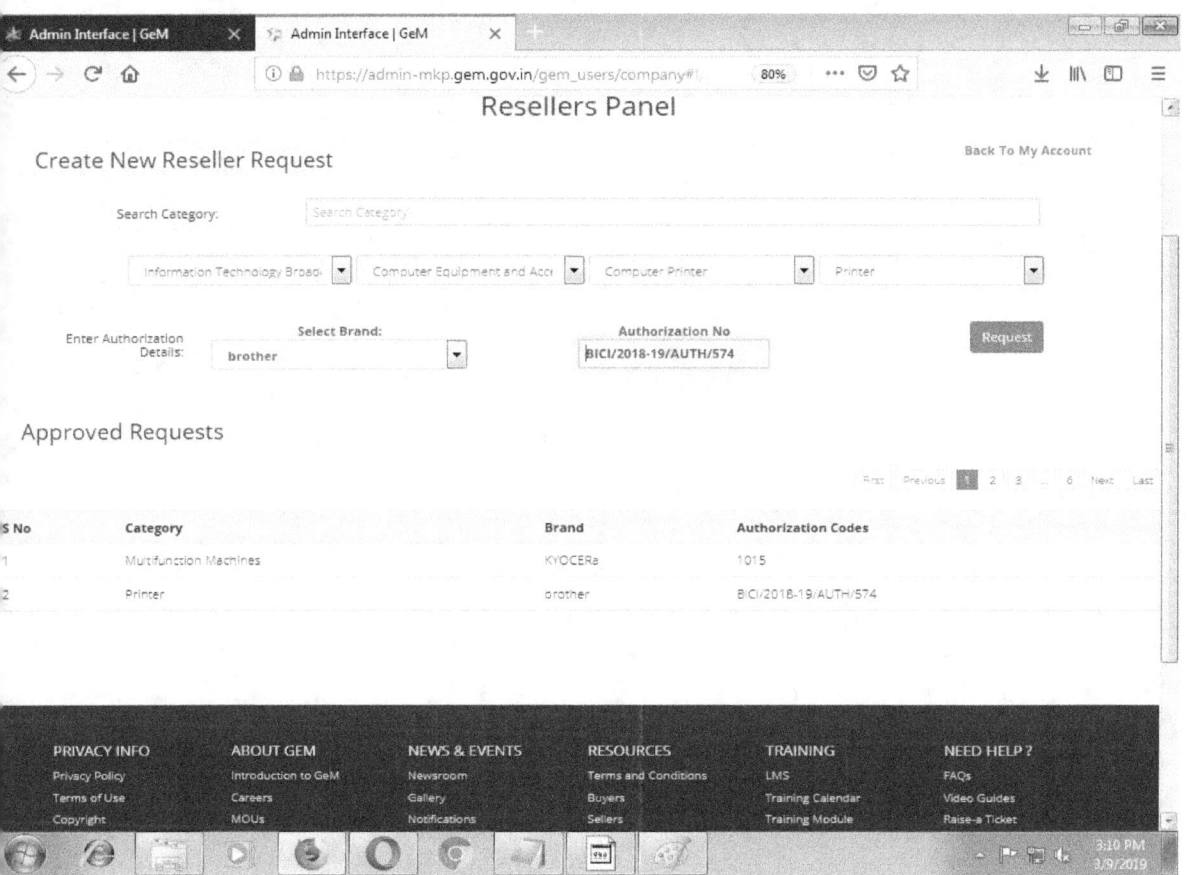

Now as you can see I choose the brand **Brother** Put in my authorization number n then we need to click on the
request button if a green bar at the top gets displayed saying **Authorization validated** means you are done
else you need to talk to OEM & or GEM. Once this is done you won't need to type in the authorization number
and the OEM name etc ever for that product you will get a dropdown while uploading and will have to just

Choose the authorization number which gets displayed there. This will keep on happening for the validity
Of the authorization for the product category, makes uploading easier.

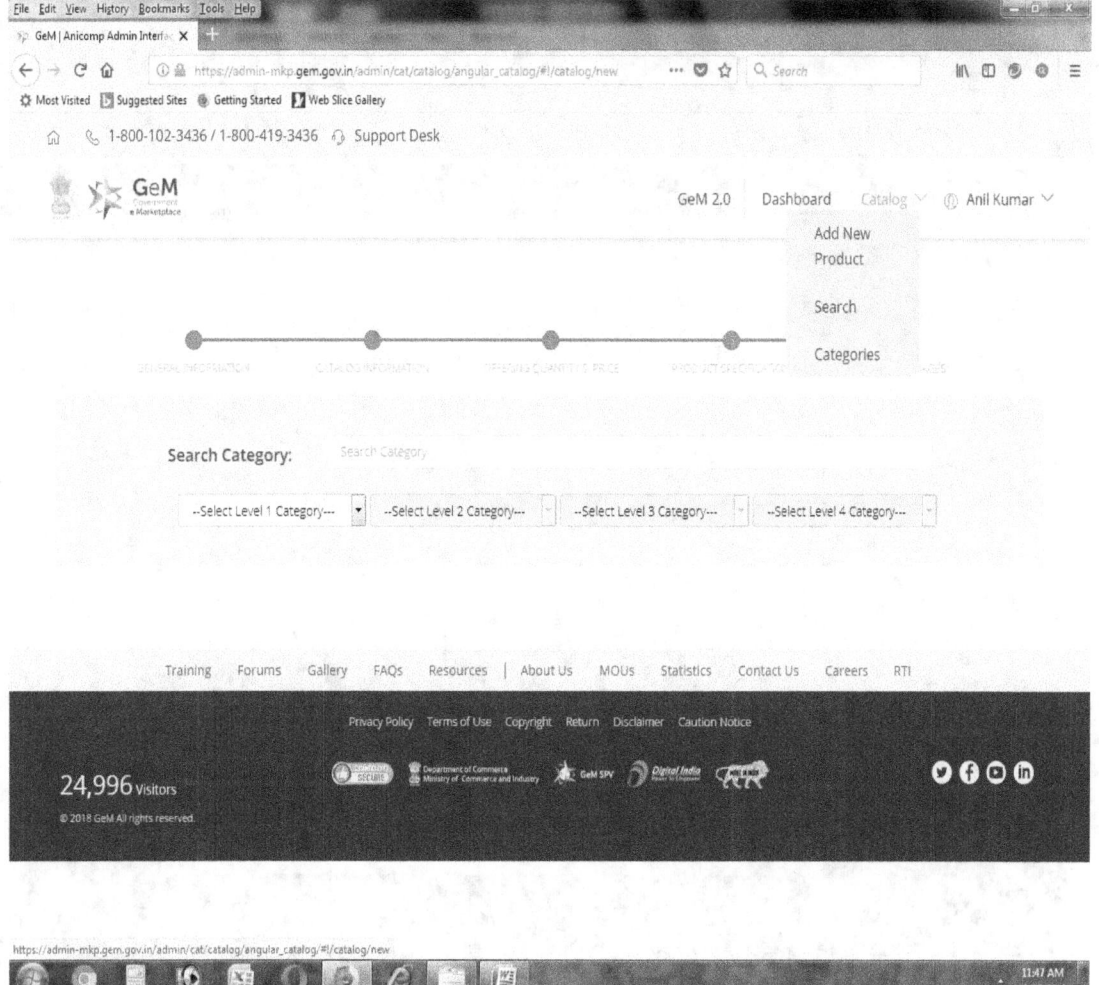

You can search for products you have uploaded under this option click on catalogue n then click search and in the search box type the brand and model click search it will be easier to look for your uploads from this option.

To add your product hover your mouse pointer over catalog and click add new product.

But now remind you again **Upload new** does not exist for most of the products.

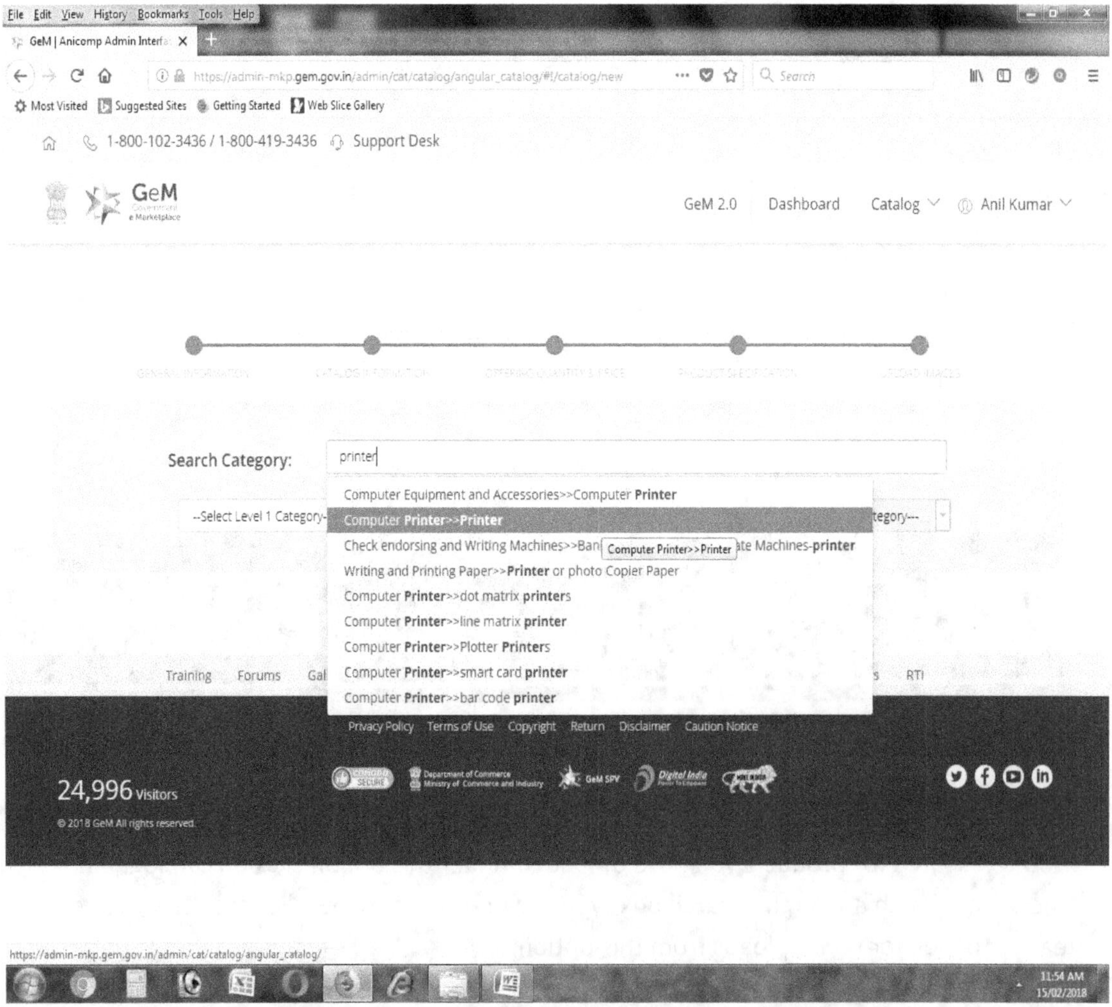

Don't search for model or Brand, ex- to upload printer type printer in the search box and choose the appropriate option. It will auto populate the product categories.

1. GENERAL INFORMATION

Product Category(Class)* Printer

Brand *
--Select--
COULDN'T FIND YOUR BRAND ? CLICK HERE TO ADD

EAN
/13 characters

Golden Parameters*

Specifications

Paper Size * --Select--

Print Speed (A4) - Mono (PPM) *

Print Speed (A4) - Color (PPM) *

Duplex Print Speed (PPM) *

On site OEM warranty (Years) * --Select--

SAVE / PROCEED

Now choose your brand if brand not there click on green text to add your brand, if you found the brand fill the rest of the information click save a new window opens showing you the products matching the information you filled in the previous page. Let's say I want to upload Brother 2321d printer, I filled the page shown above. Then I clicked save, now there 2 ways to continue from here:-

Example for upload 1

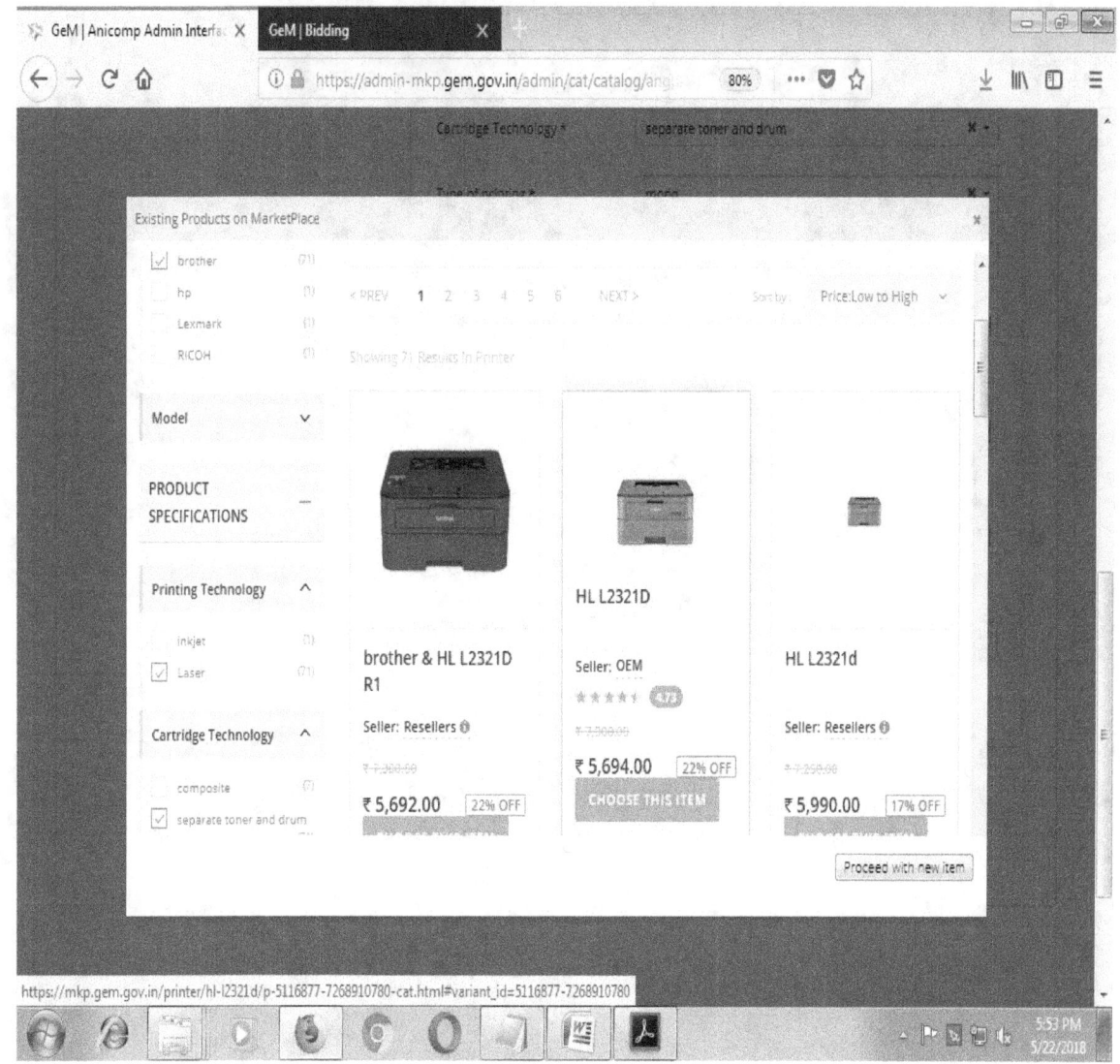

In the above image you can see its showing you what similar products are already uploaded. Hence the 1st way to upload will be to upload on someone else's upload now in order to ensure that you choose the right product choose the same model you want but before that do a right click on that model's image and a left click on open in new tab(sample image on next page).

How to check product details before upload:-

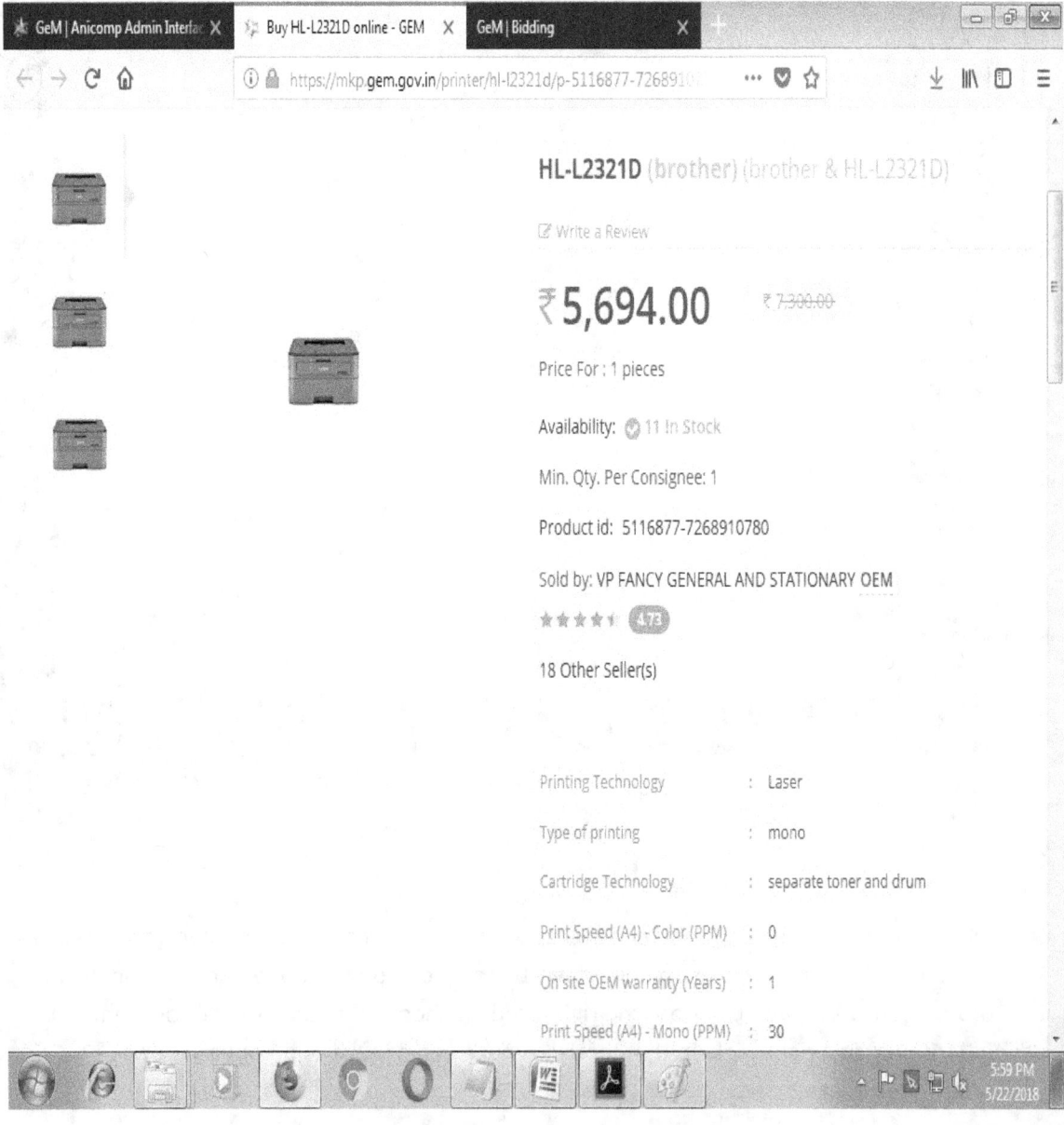

In the image above you can check the product specs, compare it from the data sheet or the brochure of the product you can also check the price range do this for multiple uploads for the model you want to upload.

Now to choose the product you have selected click on the button below its image saying choose this item, then it will only ask you to fill the stock update page which will ask you the authorization details, HSN code, stock, minimum product per order, MRP and offer price (In most cases offer price must be at least 10% less than the MRP it can be more than 10% but not less than 10%, and in some products it may be 25% so calculate accordingly)

Also a very important rule if you are a seller if you won a bid equal to or more than 25 Lakhs (25,00,000 INR) you will have to deposit an EPBG (Bank Guarantee) it's usually @2% of the total bid amount.

Uploading process GEM 3.0 no 2:- Well to upload in this way if you don't find your product in the existing products list click on new product, in this method you will have to fill Each and every thing that is being asked by GEM. Therefore things to keep handy for this process are: - Authorization letter for the brand that you are going to upload, BIS registration number (if you don't have it ask the OEM or the company Rep. to provide it to you), Price list for products to upload and do search the data sheet.pdf on google.com for the product to upload ex- Brother 2321d data sheet.pdf (make sure while searching you type the make and model no before the text data sheet.pdf) yet in most of products upload new button has been removed these days, for them you have to pair your product with someone else's upload.

Search results on next page

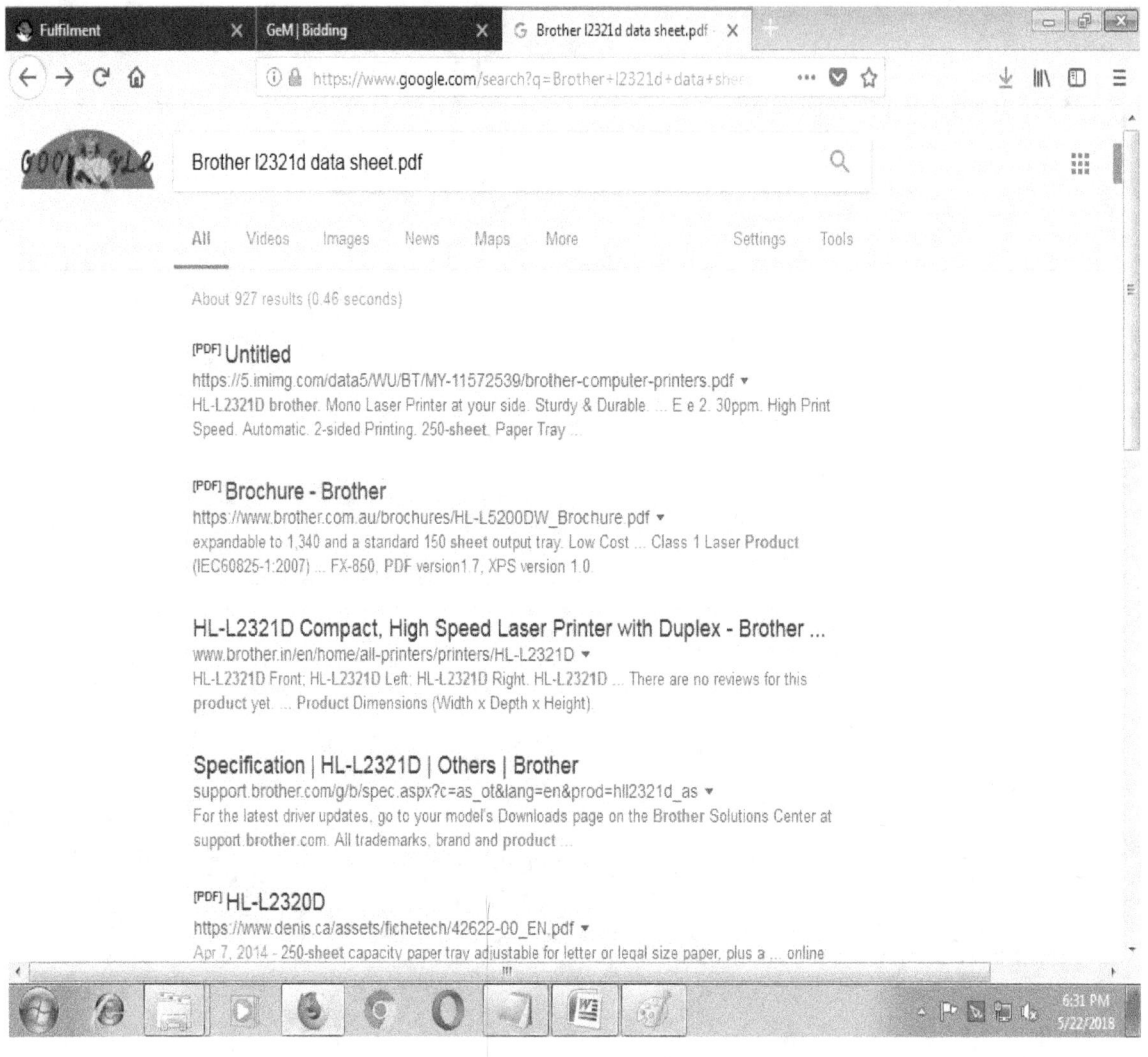

Picture above shows what came up after searching for our data sheet so we click the second one as that is from OEM and is in PDF format.

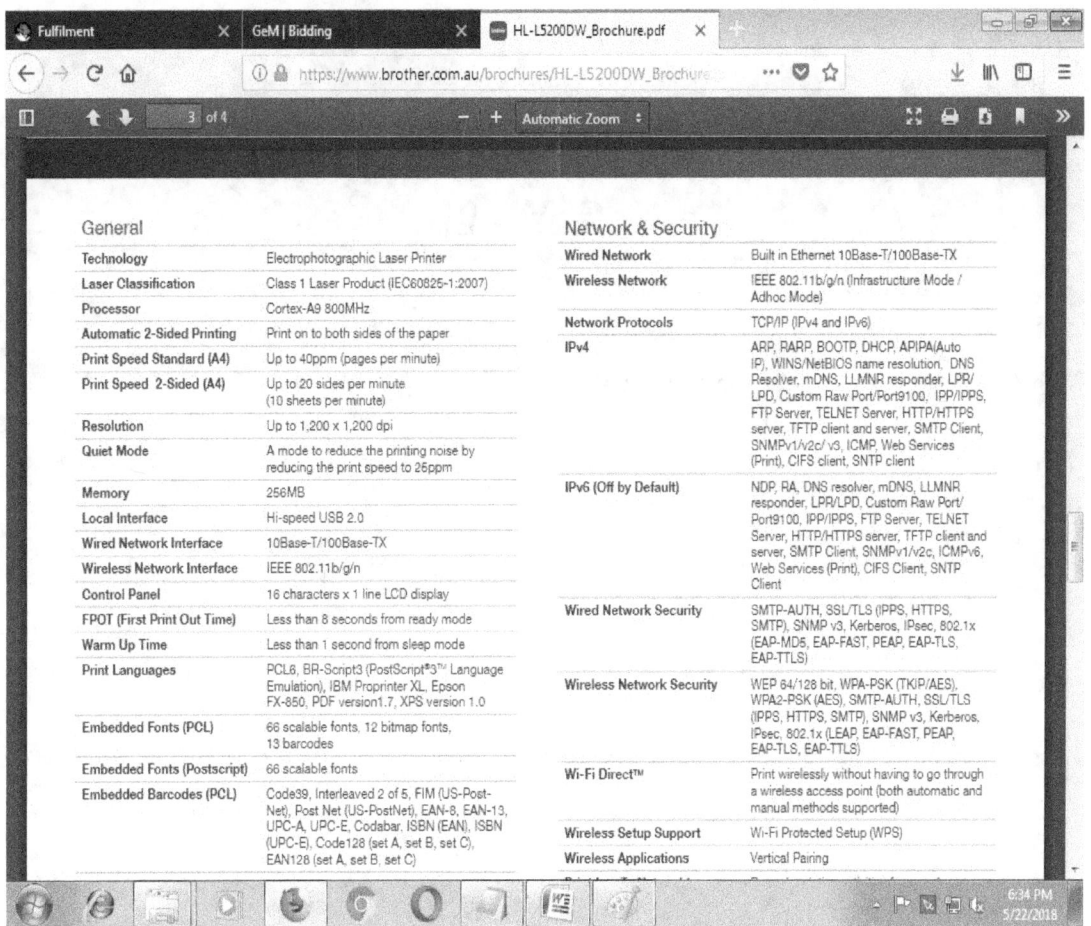

Above is the third page of the data sheet with the tech. specs. Now this document will give you the correct tech specs for you to upload products.

GEM 2.0

1) When you click GEM 2.0 at eh top of the screen

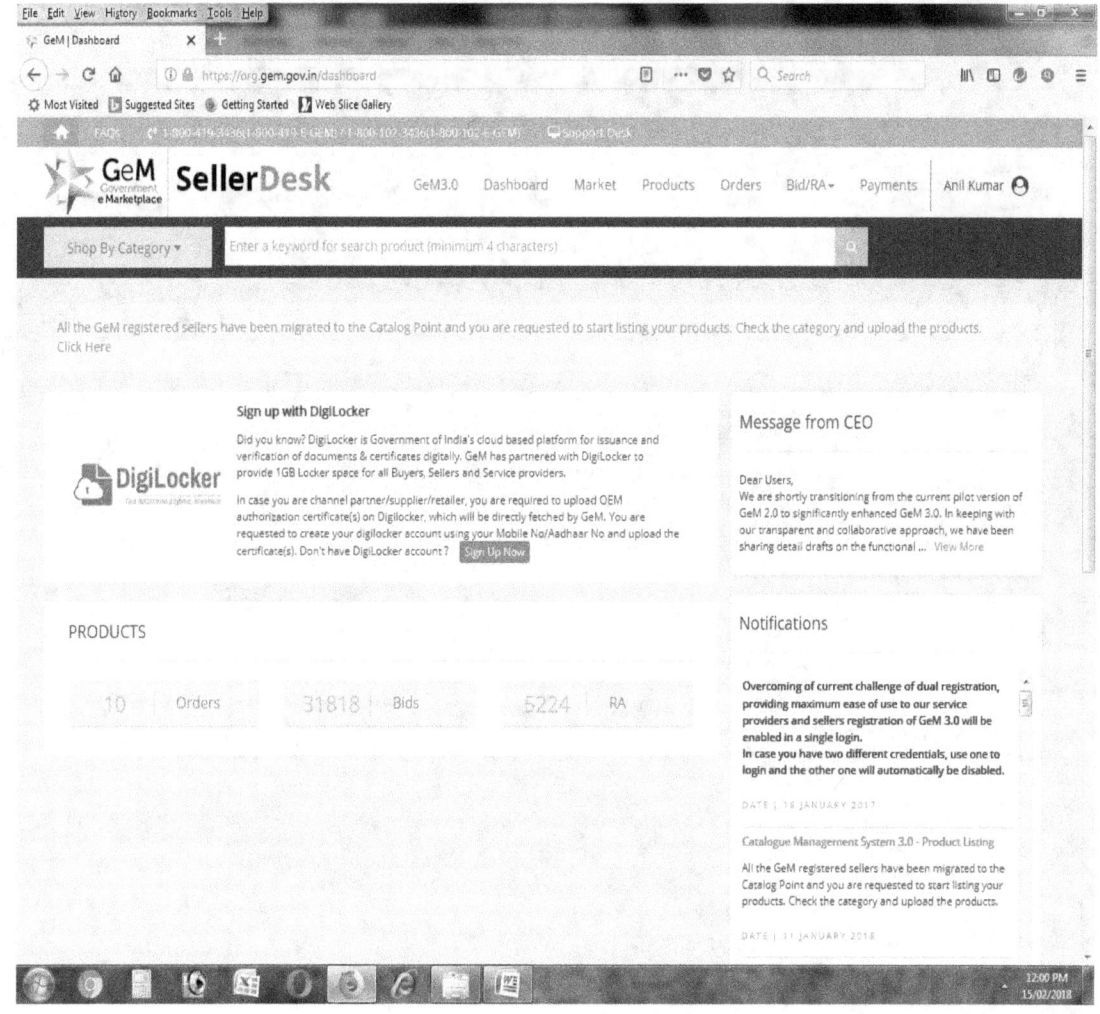

2) Orders- Here you can see the orders you received and process them

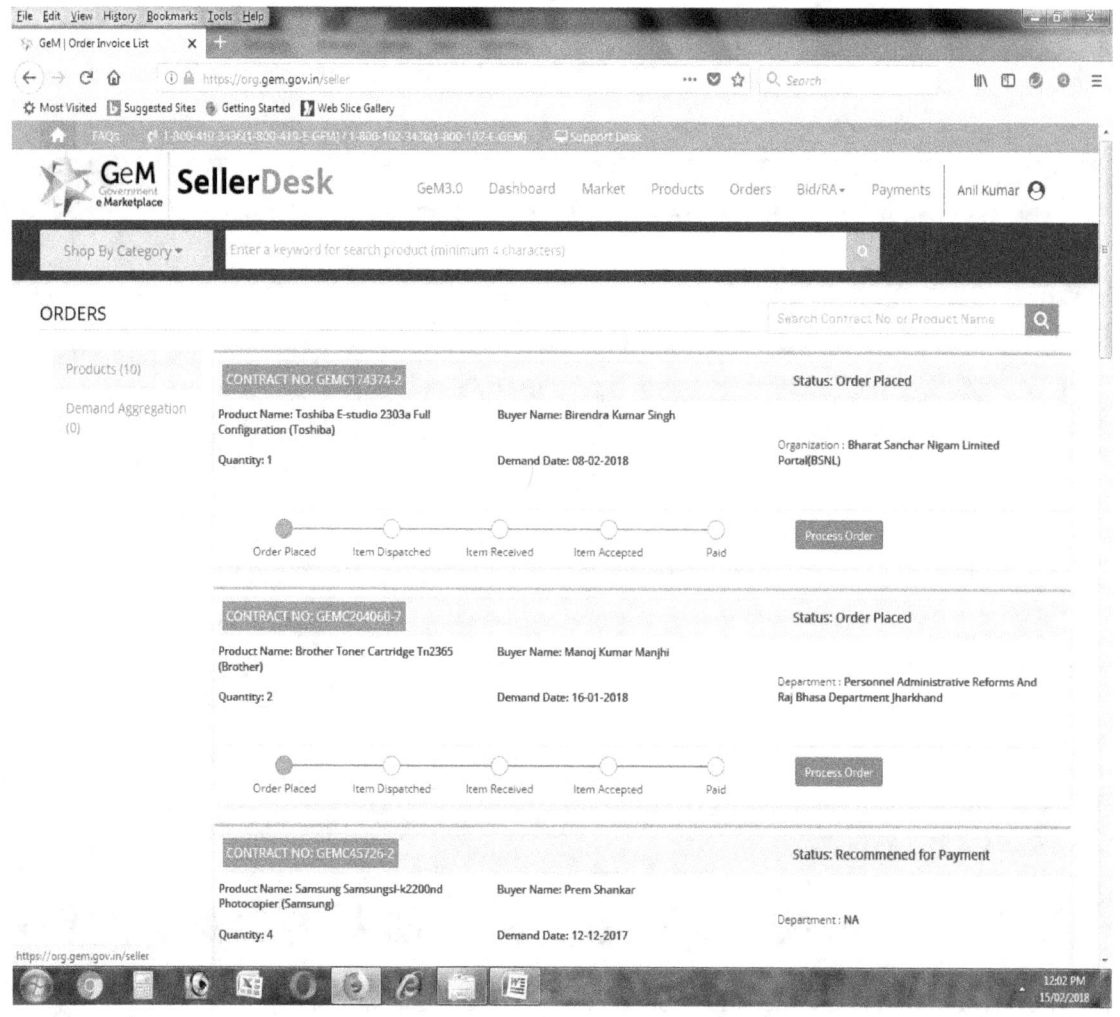

3) Payments- This tab is for confirming the payments made by the buyers.

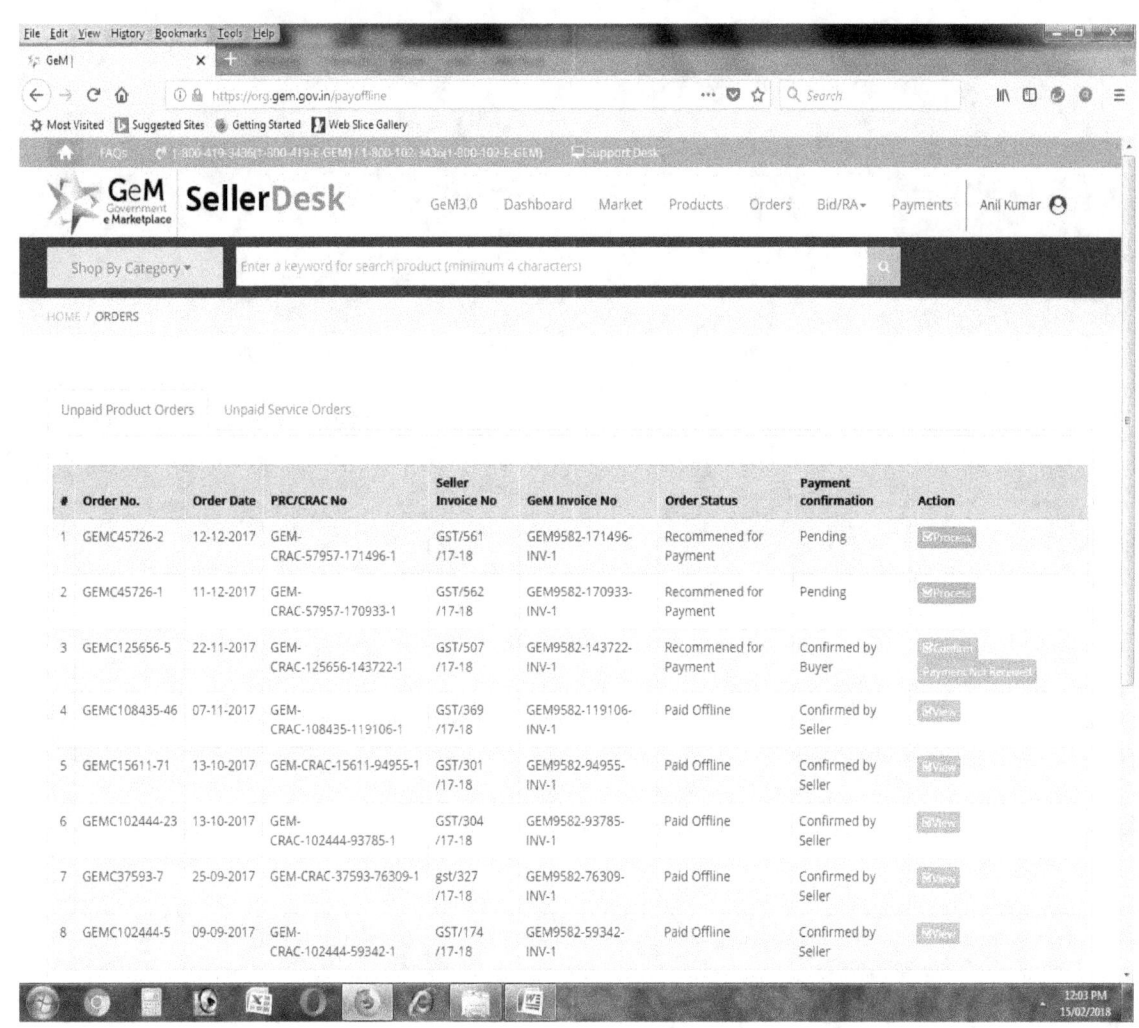

4) Bids-

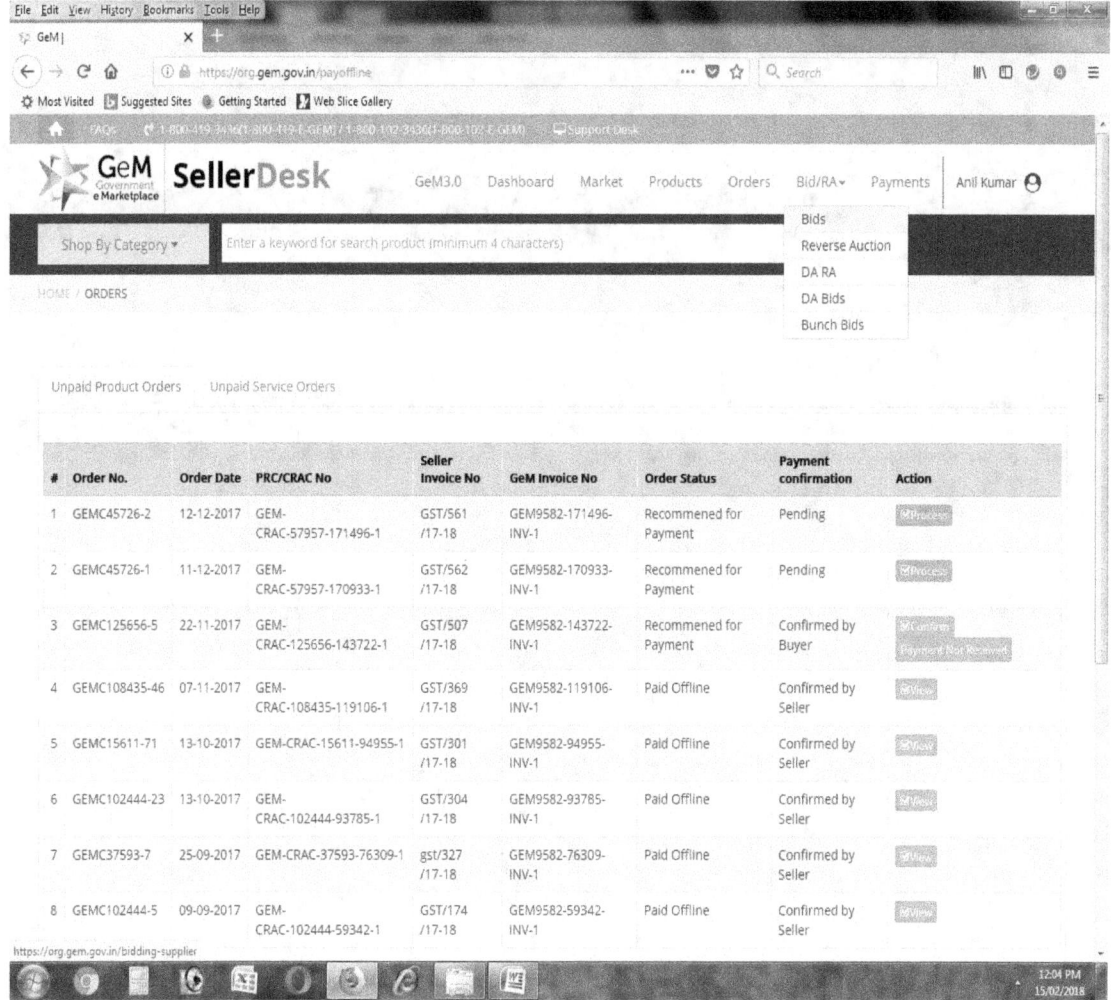

Hover your mouse over the bids link and click Bids.

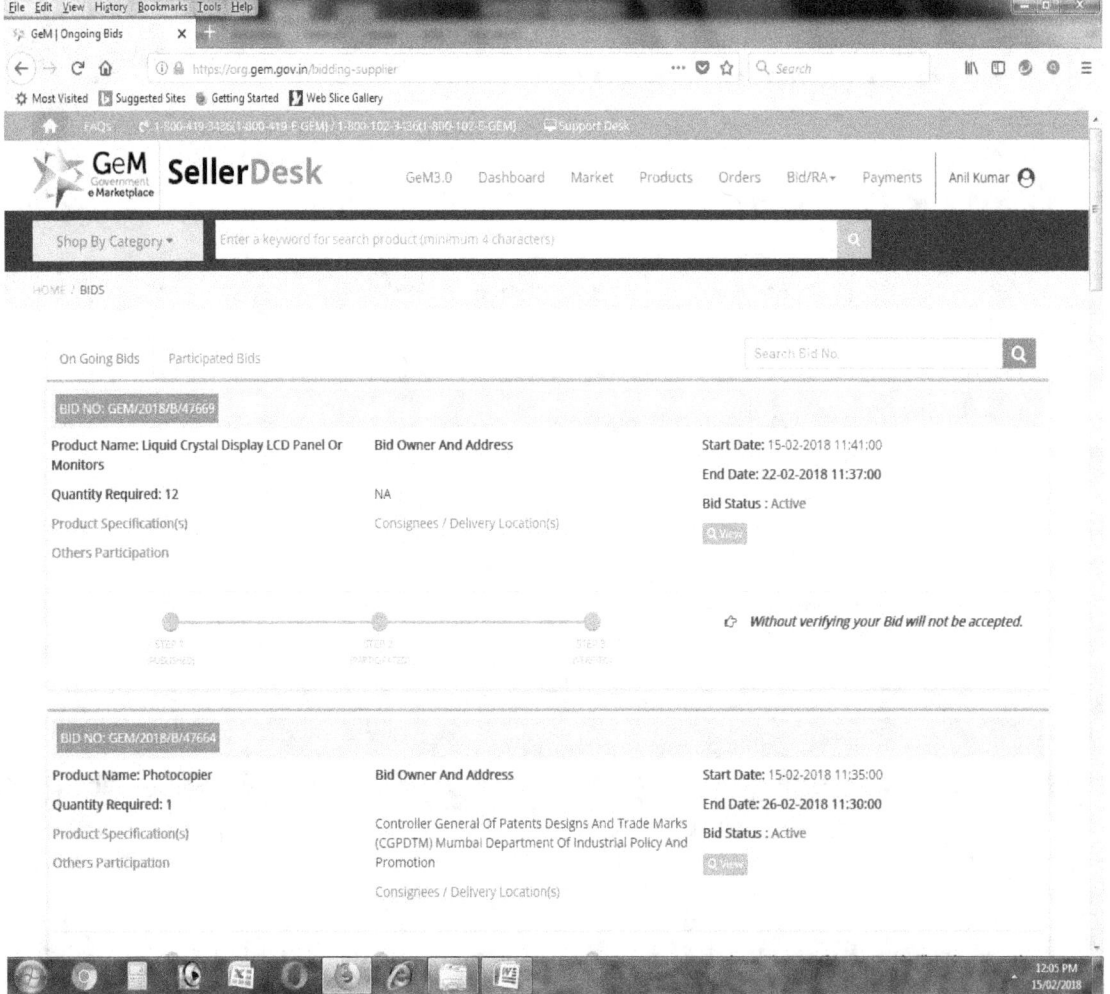

The above image is an example of bids now to see the product specs click on the link saying product specs, to find where to deliver products click consignees/delivery location, for placing bids or seeing all the info related to the bid click view

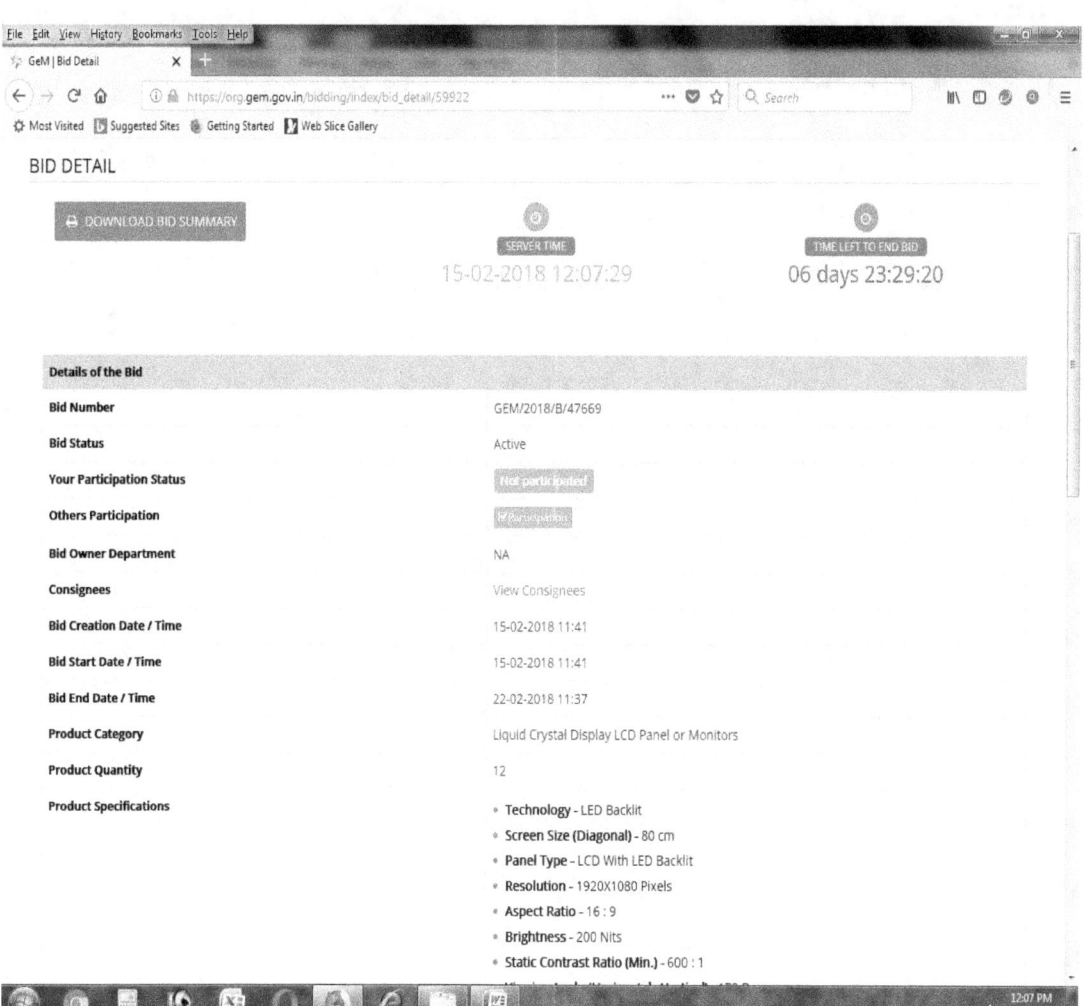

This is what we get when we click view

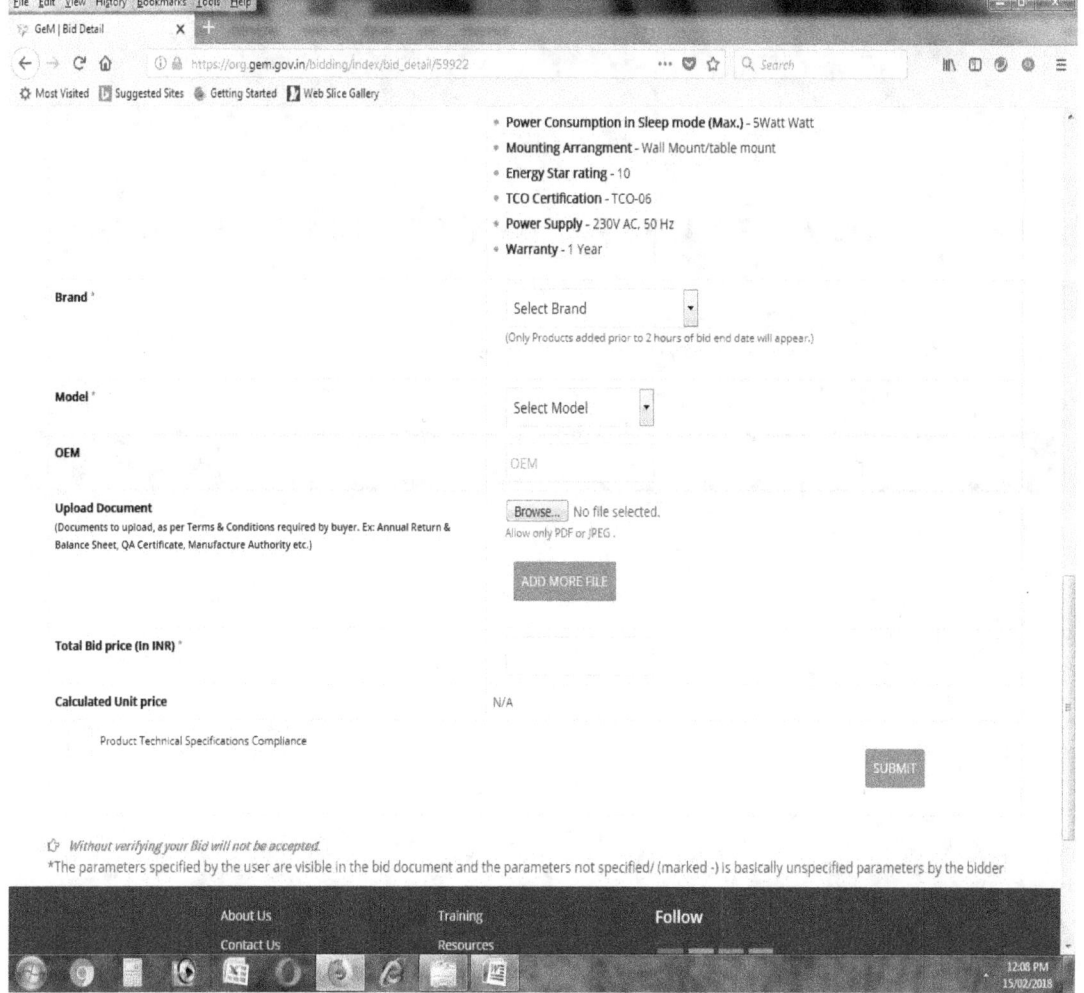

The rest of it, here you select brand, model, type in the OEM (Brand) name add any files like authorization etc, compare tech specs place the bid Note:- make sure EM-signer service is started before placing the bid, then it will ask for OTP which reaches into bosses email and **cell phone** get it type it in and submit the bid.

5) Participated Bids- These are the once where we placed a Bid and to find out whether we won it or not-
Click on the Participated bids link and you get

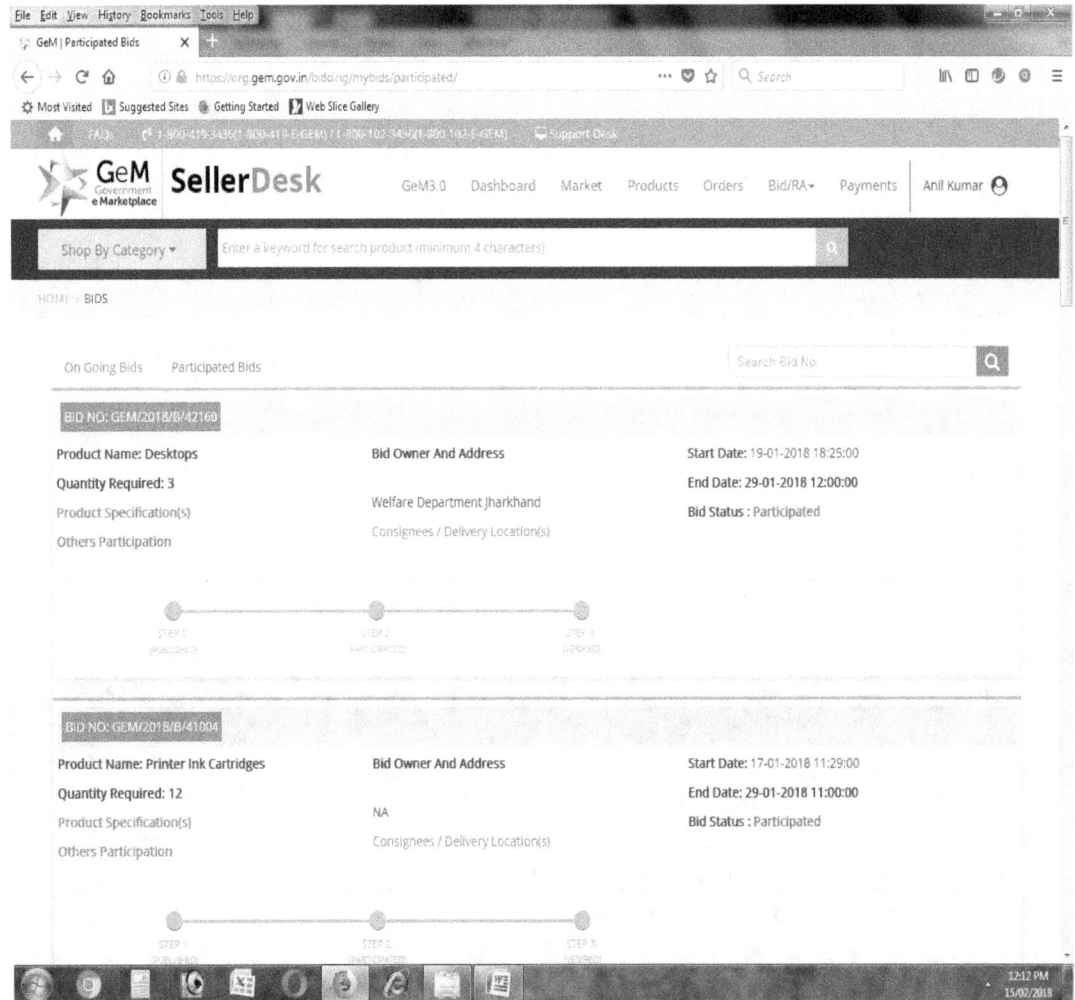

Note the green lines below means that we completed the process and to know more click others participation link.

6) RA Bid- Same as above it does not need OTP and its done in the last minutes of bids closing.

As if now 2.0 is history now and only GEM 3.0 is in effect, hence we need to focus on it more.
In GEM 3.0 Dashboard and market remain the same well most of it. New things in market,
Click on shop by category>desktop (choose the one you want, desktop in here is just for example)
As you may know old OEM Toner & desktop laptop AIO categories have been replaced so in order to search for products in the new category you need to choose the above options. Screen shot below
Once you have chosen your product category it's the old method as before product specs or make model.

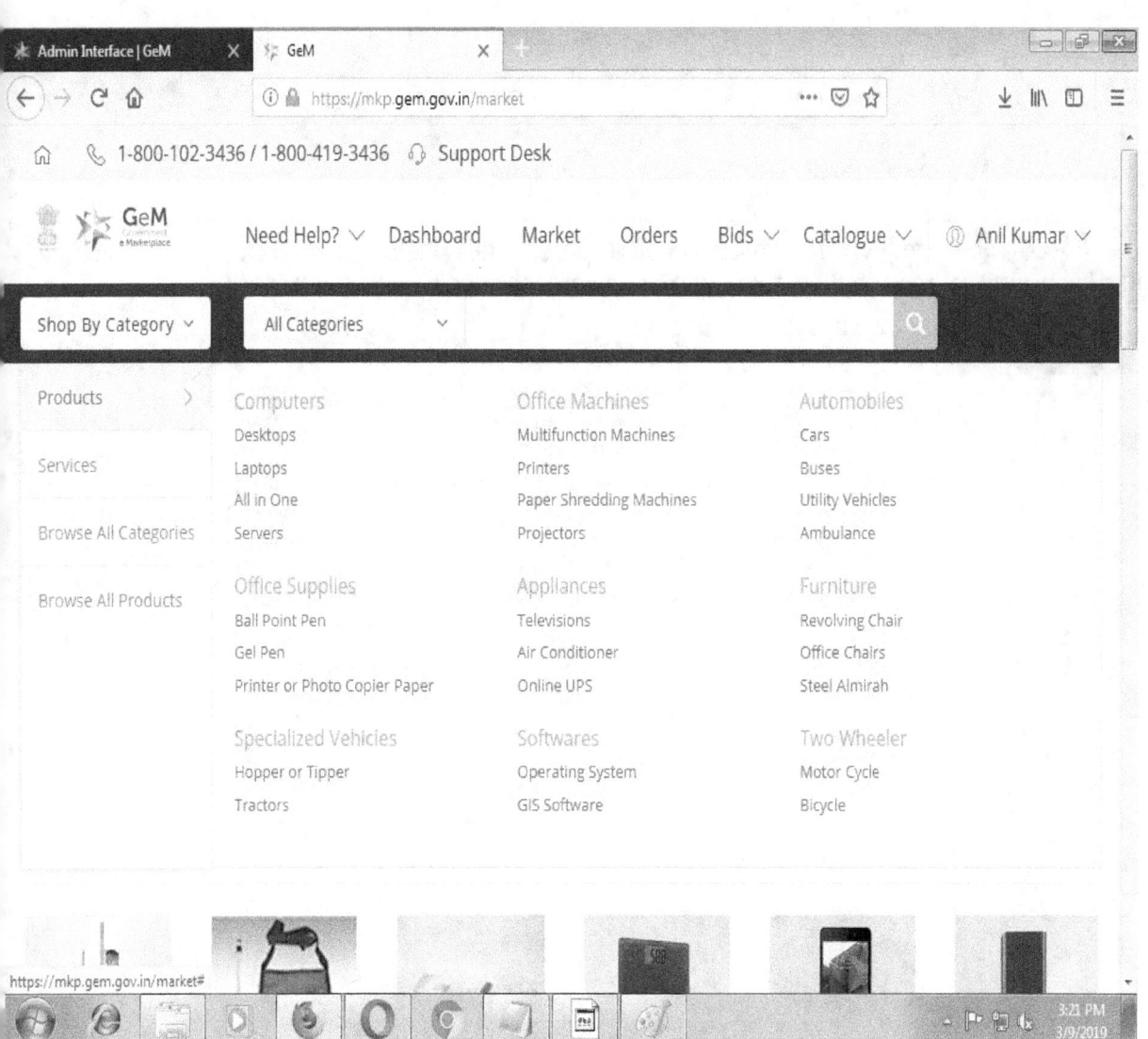

Orders :-

Now Orders were there in Gem 2.0 as well so what changed?
Well to know just that read on (first take a look on the order screen below screen shot)

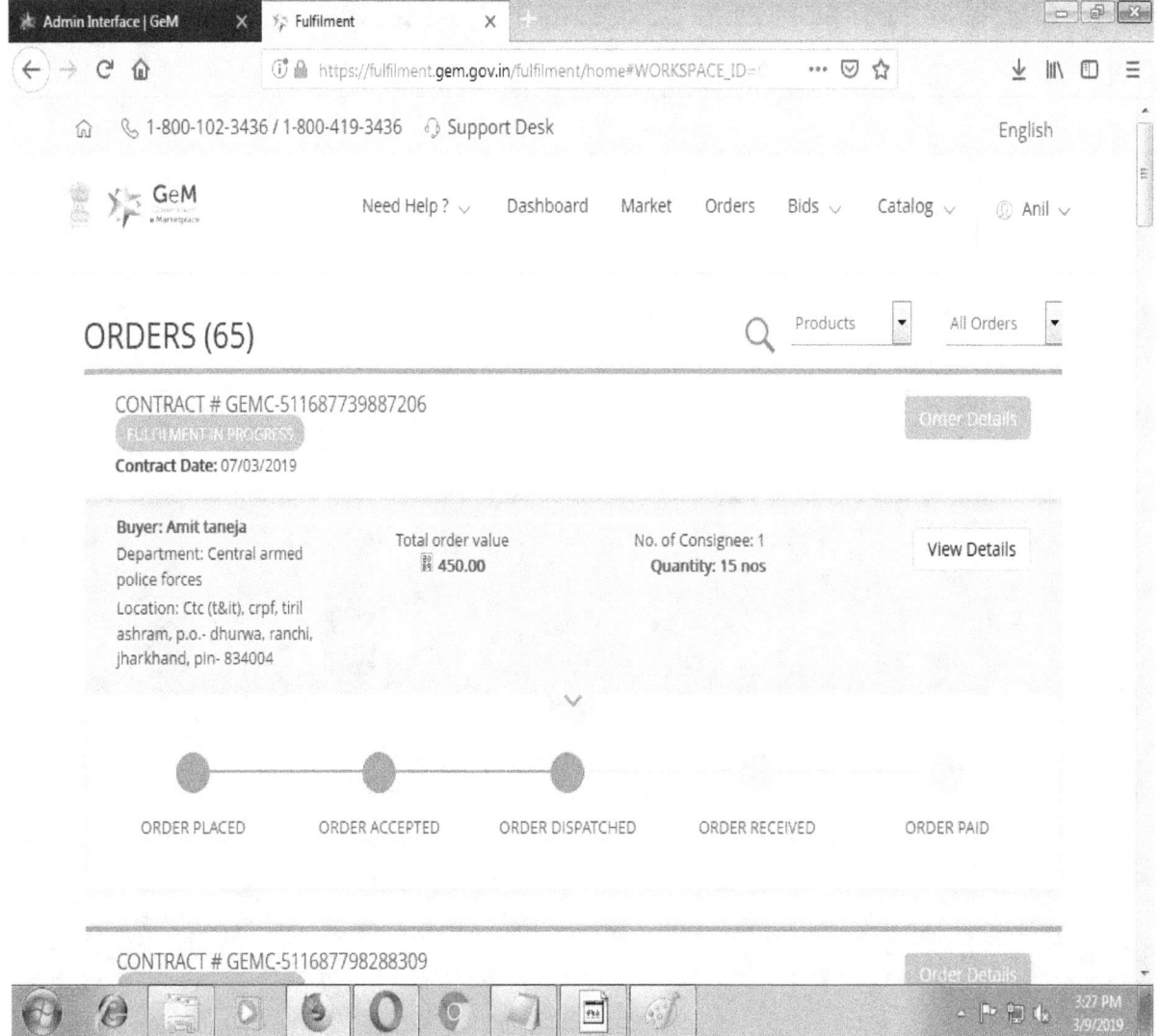

Looks pretty much the same aint it? But it's actually lot different, how?
In Gem 2.0 you just simply had to click on accept and the order will be accepted, those days
are gone now, Nowadays we need to enter **OTP** to accept an order and order that comes as a response to a bid will be **Auto accepted**,

      Question:- Ok fine I got an order what do I do, how to process the order?

      Scroll the next page to know just that....

Click on **View details** button and the page you get is in the screen-shot

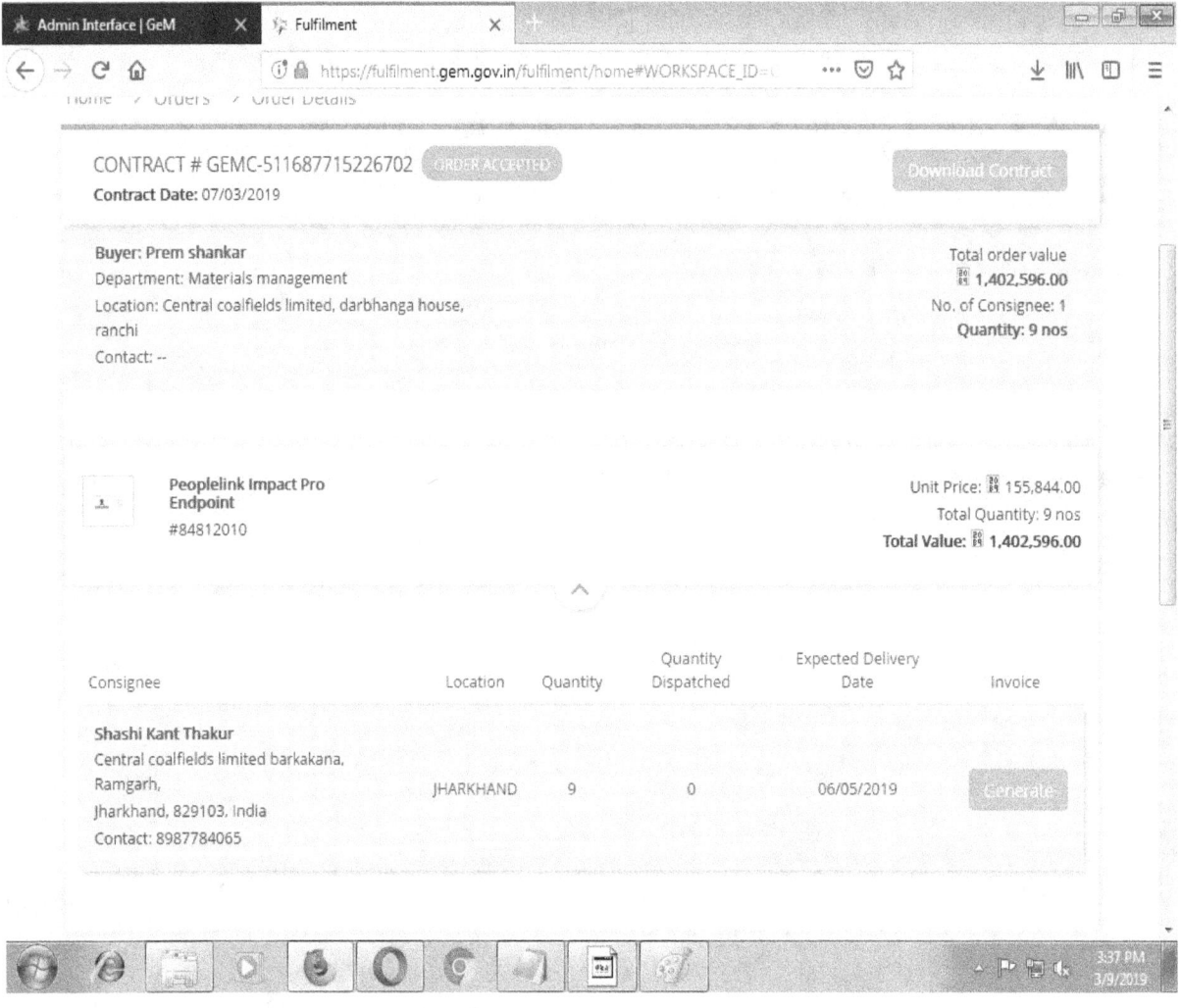

Now on this page you need to click on **generate** button once you go for it keep the GST Bill for the order handy you will need it to process the order.

All right now seller invoice no is the **GST Bill no, Invoice date** is the date of the generation of the bill or when the **GST Bill** was made, billing address is the registered address that is mentioned in your **ITR** (Income Tax return) mode of dispatch is how are you sending the product, you have to bear the shipping installation and commissioning exp within the order amount, Bank account number must be filled in your profile my account area. Now you need to fill in the order details like Quantity of product **CGST & SGST, Cess** if any and click **preview,** scroll down the page which comes up that's your GEM invoice (sorry for no screen-shot for it as I don't have any orders to process now) at the bottom of the page that opens up there is a check box place a checkmark there and click generate invoice button.

Question: - I by mistake closed the invoice it's generated but I can't see it what do I do?

Answer:- Simple solution see the next screen-shot and follow the steps

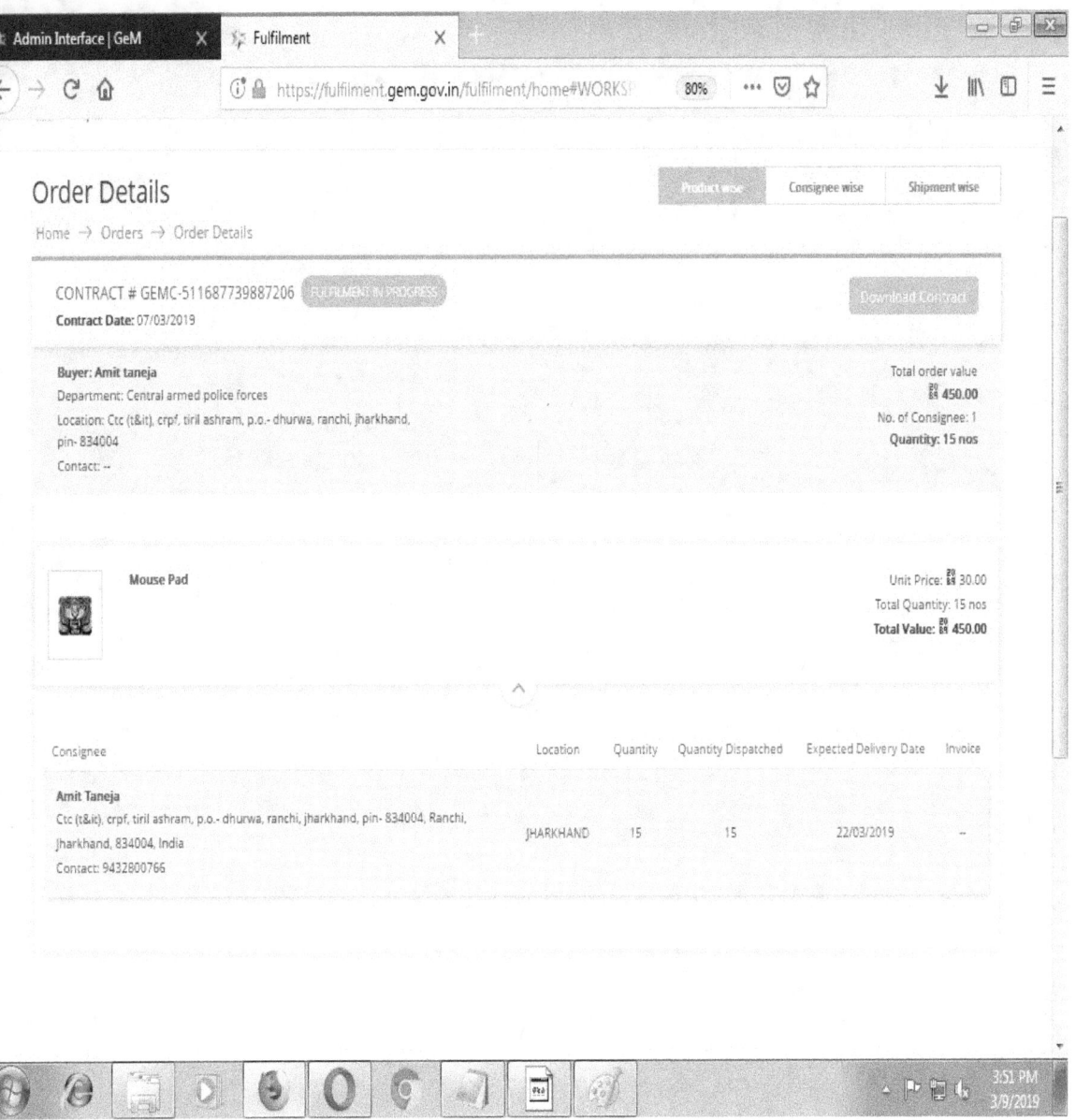

At the top right side of the page you can see three buttons you need to click the one to the extreme right which says **Shipment wise** once you do that the next page is on the next screen.

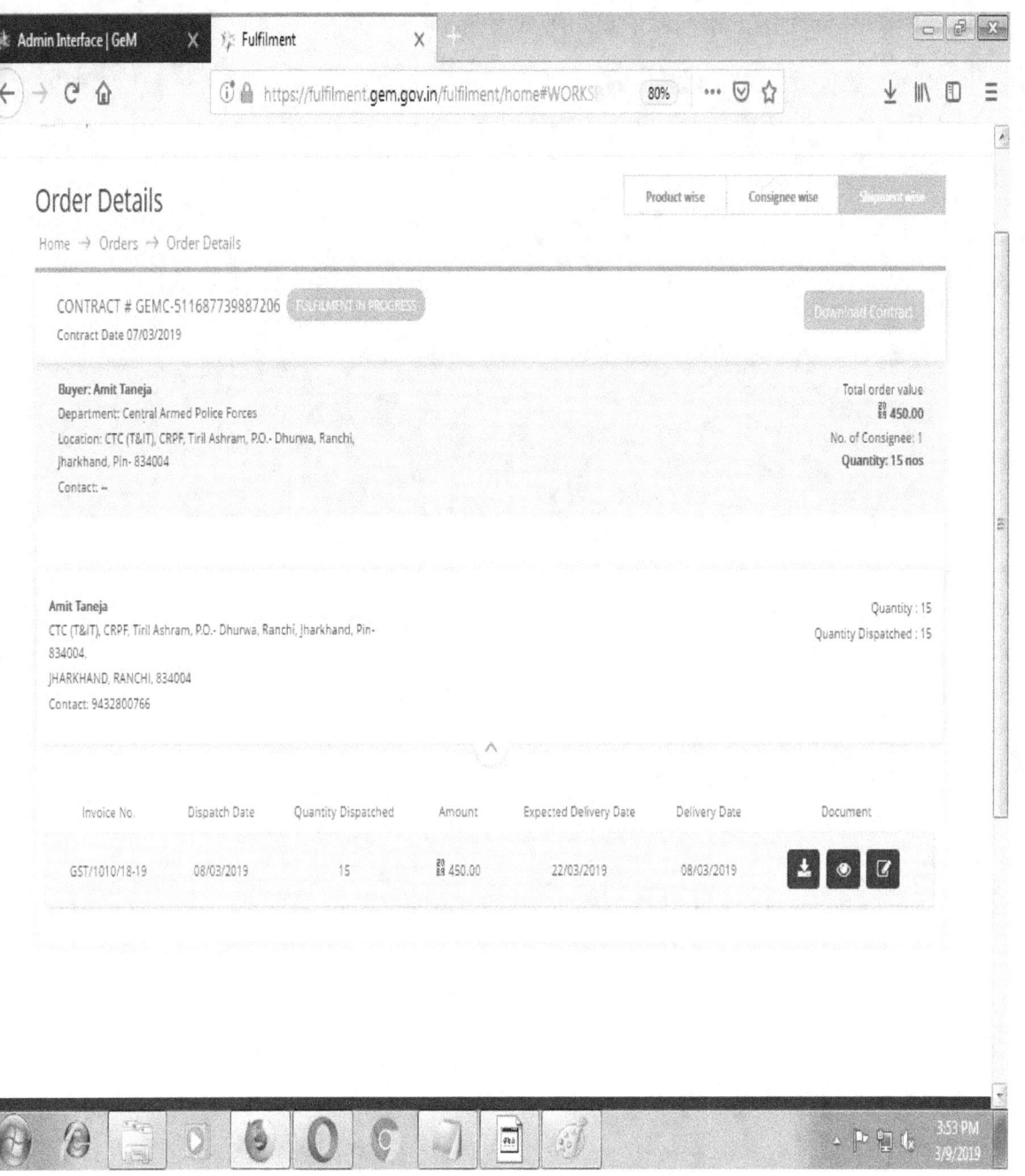

Take a look at the bottom right corner see the 3 tiny buttons first one is for downloading **the GEM Invoice**, second if you just want to take a look at it, third one is to edit Invoice. Simple aint it?

Next we'd be talking about Bids scroll down for it.

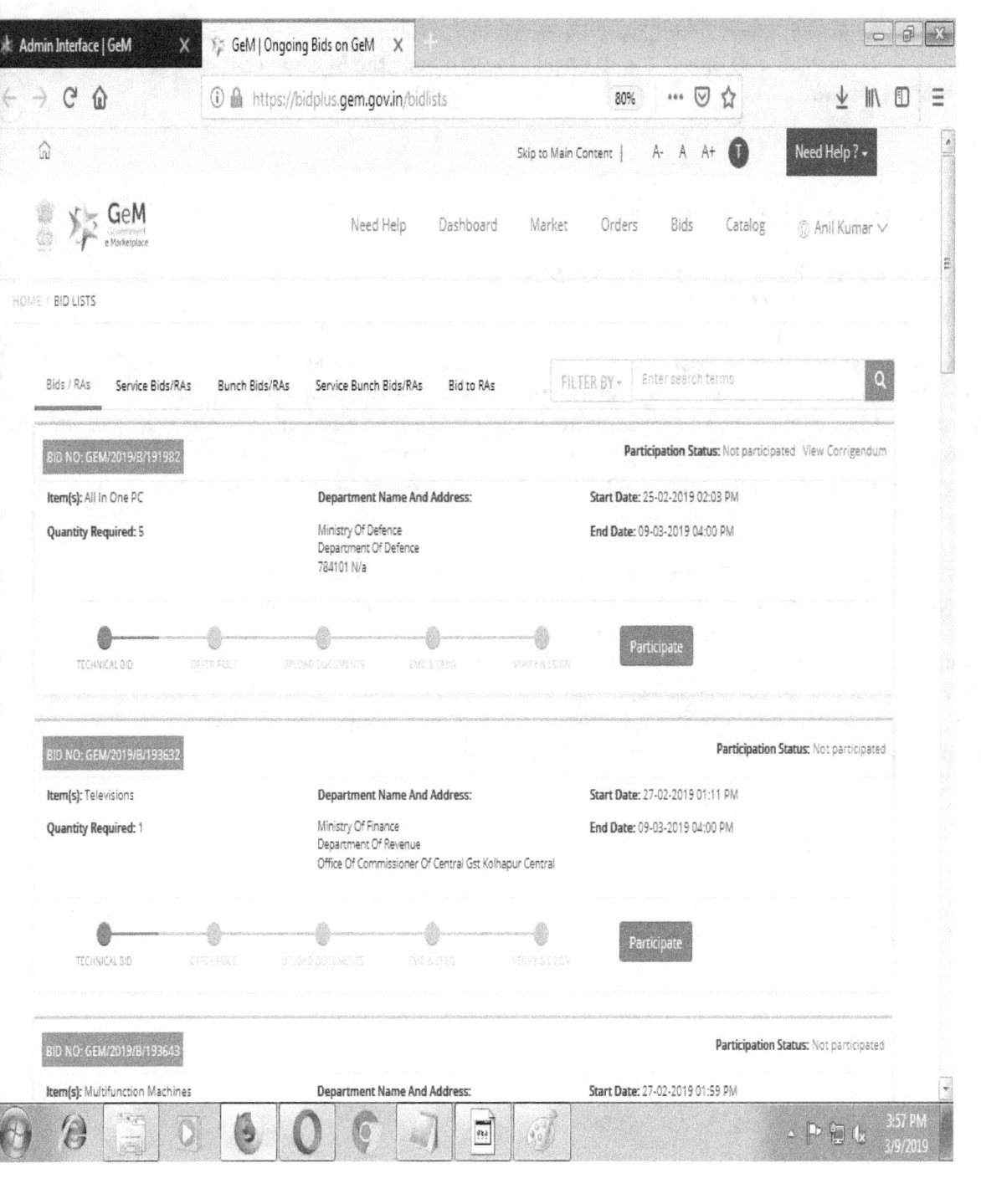

See the above screen-shot this is what Bids screen looks like in GEM 3.0 difference **now service Bids, and Bunch Service Bids & Bid to RA(Bid to RA means the Bids which have been converted into RA)**

Bidding process is the same RA doesn't need OTP.

       Note:- Want to be exempted from EMD?
           Do get MSME Certified.

      New change these days most of bids need OEM Authorization + Escalation matrix(a letter on your letterhead where you mention the names of contact persons in case the product has issues like call center number, OEM Rep phone number and your number you will need to attach a scanned copy of it into the Bid) audit report, and order copies for experience (any order copy which shows that you have supplied products to any GOVT organization or department.

      When the 3.0 was launched any product you select in a BID and click on the proceed button it got locked you won't be able to change the product without withdrawing the BID after withdrawal it took 24 hours to be able to bid again. We complained a lot and finally now we all can edit products in the Bids, if you do business on GEM and do state-wise bidding please do complain
That they need to add a feature to GEM so that we can search only the bids that belong to the state we Bid for we tried a hell lot and failed maybe you get it done will be helpful to all sellers.

Any suggestions on the content are welcomed well I hardly check my email hence recommend calling or Whatsapp on +91-909-759-3074.

www.ingramcontent.com/pod-product-compliance
Lightning Source LLC
Chambersburg PA
CBHW082121220526
45472CB00009B/2262